D1199221

WITHDRAWN

ANCIENT EARTH JOURNAL

THE EARLY CRETACEOUS:

VOLUME 1

NOTES, DRAWINGS, AND OBSERVATIONS FROM PREHISTORY

BY JUAN CARLOS ALONSO & GREGORY S. PAUL

*For Dalí, may you never lose
your sense of wonder.
Love, Dad.*

This library edition published in 2017 by Walter Foster Jr.,
an imprint of The Quarto Group
6 Orchard Road, Suite 100
Lake Forest, CA 92630

© 2015 Quarto Publishing Group USA Inc.
Published by Walter Foster Jr., an imprint of The Quarto Group
All rights reserved. Walter Foster Jr. is a registered trademark.
Artwork © Juan Carlos Alonso
Written by Juan Carlos Alonso and Gregory S. Paul
Illustrated by Juan Carlos Alonso

Distributed in the United States and Canada by
Lerner Publisher Services
241 First Avenue North
Minneapolis, MN 55401 U.S.A.
www.lernerbooks.com

First Library Edition

Library of Congress Cataloging-in-Publication Data

Names: Alonso, Juan Carlos (Graphic designer), author, illustrator. | Paul, Gregory S., author.
Title: The early Cretaceous / by Juan Carlos Alonso & Gregory S. Paul.
Other titles: Ancient Earth journal.
Description: First library edition. | Lake Forest, CA : Walter Foster Jr., an
   imprint of Quarto Publishing Group USA Inc., 2017. | Series: Ancient Earth
   journal | Audience: Ages 8+. | Includes bibliographical references and index.
Identifiers: LCCN 2017011684 | ISBN 9781942875307 (volume 1 : hardcover : alk.
   paper) | ISBN 9781942875314 (volume 2 : hardcover : alk. paper)
Subjects: LCSH: Paleontology--Cretaceous--Juvenile literature. |
   Dinosaurs--Juvenile literature. | Animals, Fossil--Juvenile literature. |
   CYAC: Prehistoric animals.
Classification: LCC QE861.5 .A427 2017 | DDC 560.177--dc23
LC record available at https://lccn.loc.gov/2017011684

Printed in USA
9 8 7 6 5 4 3 2 1

MIX
Paper from
responsible sources
FSC® C008080

Table of Contents

Forewords

Philip J. Currie, MSc, PhD, FRSC
Professor and Canada Research Chair, Dinosaur Paleobiology
University of Alberta, Edmonton, Canada

Once a dark period in the geological history of the Earth, the Early Cretaceous is rapidly becoming one of the best-understood periods of the Mesozoic Era (often called the Age of Reptiles). The Early Cretaceous is bracketed between the spectacular Late Jurassic and Late Cretaceous periods; fossil-bearing sites suggest huge changes took place in the faunas and floras during this time. In short, major transformations took place in the Early Cretaceous that signaled the beginning of the modern world. Over the last two decades, incredible fossils from this time period have been found all over the world.

Driven by the origin and rise of flowering plants, environments were starting to become more "modern" in appearance, promoting the evolution of insects, lizards, snakes, dinosaurs, birds, and mammals at unprecedented rates. However, it would still be more than 50 million years before non-avian dinosaurs would die out, along with flying reptiles and so many other animals.

As a palaeontologist who works mostly with Late Cretaceous dinosaurs, I would love to climb into a time machine and be transported back a hundred million years or so. Sitting in an Early Cretaceous forest with my pencil and notebook, camera, and sketchbook, I would try to understand the big changes that were imminent—dinosaurs were about to go into their last great flowering, with very different things happening in the northern and southern hemispheres. I would keep my eyes open for the dangerous dinosaurs, of course, especially predators such as the dog-sized Deinonychus and the giant Acrocanthosaurus. (That might be hard to do, however, because it would be so fascinating to watch the little feathered theropods like the Microraptor hunting lizards, mammals, and birds, while flocks of essentially modern birds mixed with more primitive toothed or long-tailed relatives!)

Although it will never be possible for me to travel physically back to that wonderful time, *The Early Cretaceous* has the feel of a naturalist's notebook to conjure up such illusions and dreams. I hope these wonderful images have the same effect on you!

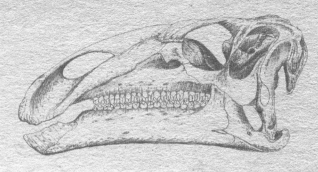

Matthew T. Mossbrucker

Director & Chief Curator

Morrison Natural History Museum, Morrison, Colorado

So that's what they think dinosaurs looked like? I have seen this scenario play out in museum exhibits on scores of occasions. Curious visitors introduced to life history via art. This synergy between paleontologists, who are charged with the study of fossil life forms, and specially trained artists is vital for intuitively communicating past life on earth.

Those of us who are charged with interpreting fossils for the masses have come to rely on this special type of artist, the "paleoartist," to help us resurrect animals and plants from the deep recesses of time. Paleoartists are the unsung heroes of science literacy. Their vital skills translate the inanimate remains of long-dead creatures once again into living beasts. They inspire a connection between our world and the countless ecosystems that have come and gone before us.

Perhaps nothing stirs the imagination like dinosaurs—monstrous and exotic forms brought to life through the imagination of artistic scientists like Juan Carlos Alonso and Gregory S. Paul. This book is a wonderful blend of imagination and reality and a testament to the powerful partnership between art and science.

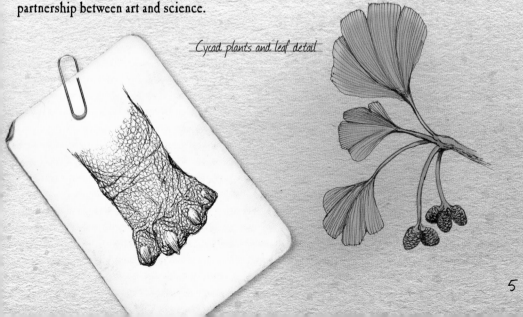

Cycad plants and leaf detail

Introduction

I magine stepping back in time 120 million years to the Early Cretaceous period and walking around on an earth similar to today's, yet in many regards, almost alien.

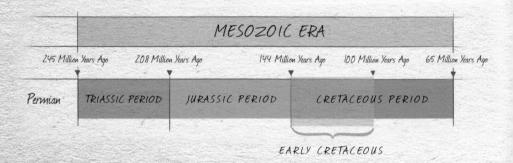

MESOZOIC ERA

245 Million Years Ago   208 Million Years Ago   144 Million Years Ago   100 Million Years Ago   65 Million Years Ago

Permian   TRIASSIC PERIOD   JURASSIC PERIOD   CRETACEOUS PERIOD

EARLY CRETACEOUS

The Early Cretaceous is the last period of the Mesozoic Era, or "the age of the reptiles." The earth is undergoing monumental changes; the once giant supercontinent is slowly drifting apart. The tectonic plates are tearing apart along a great fiery rift, forming the early North Atlantic Ocean. South America and Africa are still partly attached to one another, while close by Antarctica, Australia, and India are bundled into one continent.

A massive shallow sea covers large areas, turning Europe into an archipelago of islands similar to today's Indonesia. The great tropical Tethys Ocean divides Asia from the southern continents and the vast Pacific Ocean is the largest it will ever be.

As you travel through the Early Cretaceous, you will experience warm temperatures throughout most of the world. Seasons consist of a dry and a wet period. Approaching the poles, winters are dark and very cold. You will see glaciers gracing some highlands, especially in the southernmost areas. As you cross the center of the continents, you will encounter endless arid deserts, making your journey difficult, if not impossible. Areas of abundant plant life are widespread, with the ground covered in waist-high ferns forming broad prairies in drier flatlands.

As you travel through forests, you will see short cycads, gingko trees, and enormous canopies of towering conifers. Small flowering shrubs—the first to appear on the earth—decorate the banks of streams and creeks. You can't walk through fields of grass nor can you see hardwood trees, including oak or walnut, as they haven't evolved yet. A lot of the animal life will look familiar to you. Small bodies of water are home to frogs, turtles, and salamanders.

You might find lizards and rodent-sized mammals scurrying through the underbrush as well as burrowing into the ground. The insects look familiar too; you will spot dragonflies, flies, fleas, roaches, social termites, wasps, and moths. In many ways,

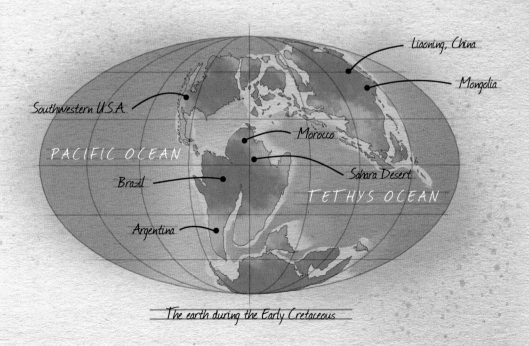

The earth during the Early Cretaceous

the Early Cretaceous will remind you of several places on earth today. But in other ways, it is an incredibly different world.

Much of the wildlife of the Early Cretaceous period is simply extraordinary! Animals have adapted for survival in a dinosaur-dominated environment so savage that it's unsafe for people to move about unless they are armed.

Deadly two-legged, long-tailed predators the length of a city bus and swifter than any human roam freely, each capable of swallowing a man whole. (It's no wonder that some herbivorous dinosaurs are armored like tanks!) Others are land whales weighing up to 100 tons and measuring five stories tall! These creatures move in huge herds, wrecking the umbrella-shaped conifers they feed upon. Yet other big herbivorous dinosaurs look like crosses between massive cattle and ducks, with flat beaks designed for tearing into plants.

Not all of the Early Cretaceous dinosaurs are big, however. In fact, most are fairly small and often feathered like birds. Most of the small dinosaurs are beaked plant-eaters and fast on their two legs. Many are bipedal predators. Some have sickle-shaped razor claws on their inner toes used to disembowel their prey. The dinosaurs most closely related to birds have wings on both of their arms and legs that they use to fly between trees and pounce on prey from above. Birds as we now know them today are just beginning to appear. They often live in enormous flocks, giving some

Pinecones

Conifer branch and needles

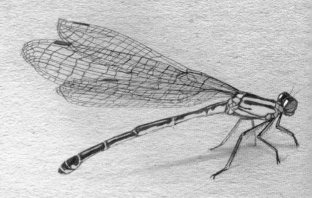

stiff competition to the flying pterosaurs that had long ruled the skies. Pterosaurs are growing larger, sporting enormous head crests and shorter tails.

Now imagine living alongside these animals, recording and sketching every possible detail of their lives in your journal. The premise of this book is to bring these magnificent animals to life for you through art and science. Discover the Early Cretaceous world and its life through new eyes, and get to know the personalities of each species. Discover how dinosaurs learned to fly as they developed wings. See how some dinosaurs survived polar blizzards, while others lived through desert heat. This journal gives you a visual guide to what it must have been like to experience possibly the strangest wildlife the earth has ever seen and may never see again.

Welcome to the Early Cretaceous.

The Theropods

Few animals, living or extinct, inspire as much awe and terror as the theropod dinosaurs. Think what it would be like to be in the Early Cretaceous and encounter an animal 40 feet long with a head the size of your body and sharp teeth 8 inches long. Its small eyes are fixed on you as it catches your scent. You try to run, but it's much faster than you. You try to hide, but its highly developed olfactory senses can smell you no matter where you are. You are no match for the greatest predator to ever exist. Luckily, an encounter such as this will never happen, but the descendants of the great theropod dinosaurs live among us in the form of birds.

Theropods, meaning "beast-footed," are a diverse group of dinosaurs that lived throughout the Mesozoic Era. They are classified as saurischian dinosaurs, or "lizard-hipped" (because of the structure of their hips), and are mostly recognized for being bipedal. Theropod species ranged in size from miniscule, 12 inches in length, to the super predators measuring over 50 feet long.

With a few exceptions, theropod bodies were slender with longer hind limbs, shorter forelimbs, and a long tail. Their hands usually had three fingers and were used for

6 feet

3 feet

specialized functions such as flight or grasping prey; in some cases, they were atrophied to the point of near uselessness. Their feet contained four toes, three of which made contact with the ground and were used for walking and running. Theropod skeletons were constructed of thin-walled, hollow bones with relatively large skulls. Most theropod skulls have several holes in their structure; these holes are called "fenestra," and their purpose was to make the heads lighter, sometimes allowing for larger and heavier teeth.

Most theropods were carnivorous, feeding on other dinosaurs, insects, and fish; others were herbivorous, feeding only on plants. Some were omnivorous, feeding both on plants and meat. While all are fascinating, it is the carnivorous theropods that inspire the most awe. With an arsenal of weapons, including talons, razor-sharp claws, and serrated teeth designed to cut flesh, these are the most fearsome creatures ever to inhabit earth. Today, birds are the only remaining descendant of the theropods; so the tiny sparrow flying outside your window is a distant cousin of the great Tyrannosaurus.

Like birds, theropods were born from round or oval-shaped, hard-shelled eggs. The hatchling would use a small, hard growth on its nose called an "egg tooth" to break its way out of the shell. This egg tooth would fall off its nose soon after emerging from the egg. And, also like birds, several species are known to have cared for their young by feeding and protecting them.

Theropods were also diverse in their skin textures and coverings. Some bodies were covered in a fine filament, called "protofeathers," some in a mosaic of smooth and bumpy scales, and others were covered in feathers and even had fully functioning wings.

The Theropods of the Early Cretaceous

Following the Jurassic Period, apex predators like Allosaurus and Torvosaurus were replaced by Acrocanthosaurus atokensis and Carcharodontosaurus saharicus. Bigger, stronger species evolved to fill their role at the top of the food chain. While some predators became larger, new species like Utahraptor ostrommaysorum, with its sickle-shaped killing claw, also found their place in the Early Cretaceous. Flying raptor dinosaurs continued to evolve with species like Microraptor gui, which used wings on both its legs and arms to glide through trees and capture prey.

Egg tooth

Theropod hatchling

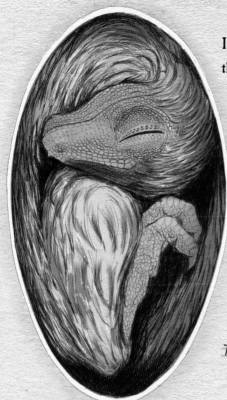

In some cases, it was the adaptation to specific prey that made the theropods unique. Baryonyx walkeri developed strong muscular arms with hooked claws and a long snout with conical teeth all designed to grasp fish. Not all adaptations were about hunting; Concavenator corcovatus evolved strange hump structures on its back used as a display to attract mates. This was an amazing period in earth's history. In the following pages you will experience these animals in detail, species by species, and witness the theropods of the Early Cretaceous.

Theropod inside *egg*

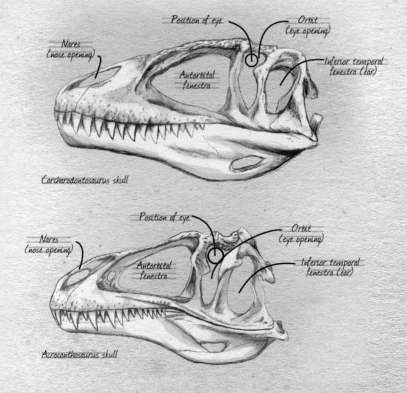

Position of eye

Orbit
(eye opening)

Nares
(nose opening)

Antorbital
fenestra

Inferior temporal
fenestra (ear)

Carcharodontosaurus skull

Position of eye

Orbit
(eye opening)

Nares
(nose opening)

Antorbital
fenestra

Inferior temporal
fenestra (ear)

Acrocanthosaurus skull

Acrocanthosaurus atokensis

Location Observed: Oklahoma, Texas, and Wyoming, United States

Family: Carcharodontosauridae

Length: 35 feet (11 meters)

Height: 14 feet (4.5 meters)

Weight: 4.4 tons

Temperament: Solitary, very aggressive

Dermal growth on head

Elongated dorsal spines form a sail along back and top of tail

Powerfully built small hands and arms

Muscular legs

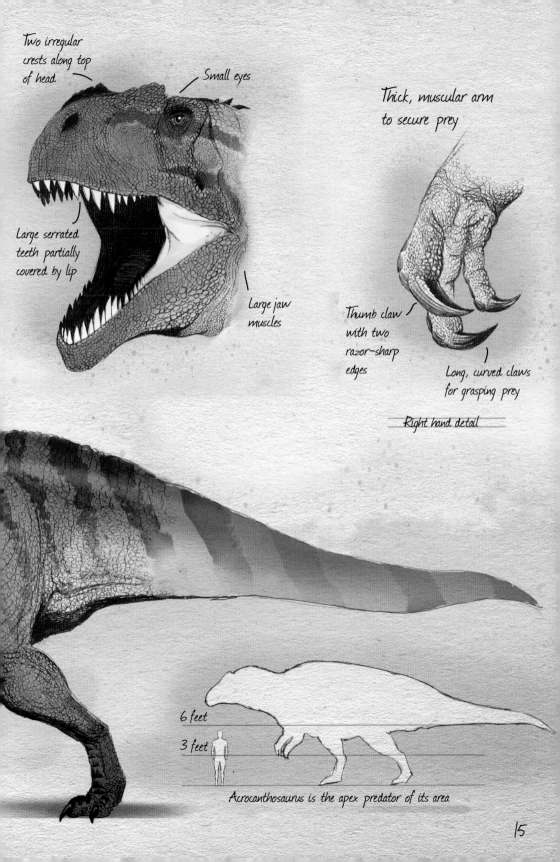

Two irregular crests along top of head

Small eyes

Large serrated teeth partially covered by lip

Large jaw muscles

Thick, muscular arm to secure prey

Thumb claw with two razor-sharp edges

Long, curved claws for grasping prey

Right hand detail

6 feet

3 feet

Acrocanthosaurus is the apex predator of its area

Baryonyx walkeri

Location Observed: Southeast England, Weald Clay

Family: Spinosauridae

Length: 25 feet (7.5 meters)

Height: 7 feet (2.1 meters)

Weight: 1.2 tons

Temperament: Solitary, territorial, aggressive

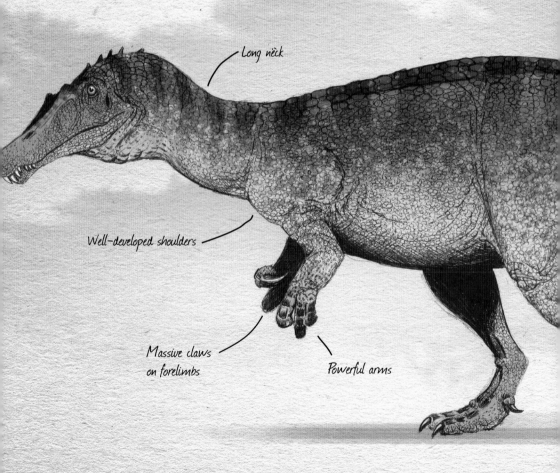

Long neck

Well-developed shoulders

Massive claws
on forelimbs

Powerful arms

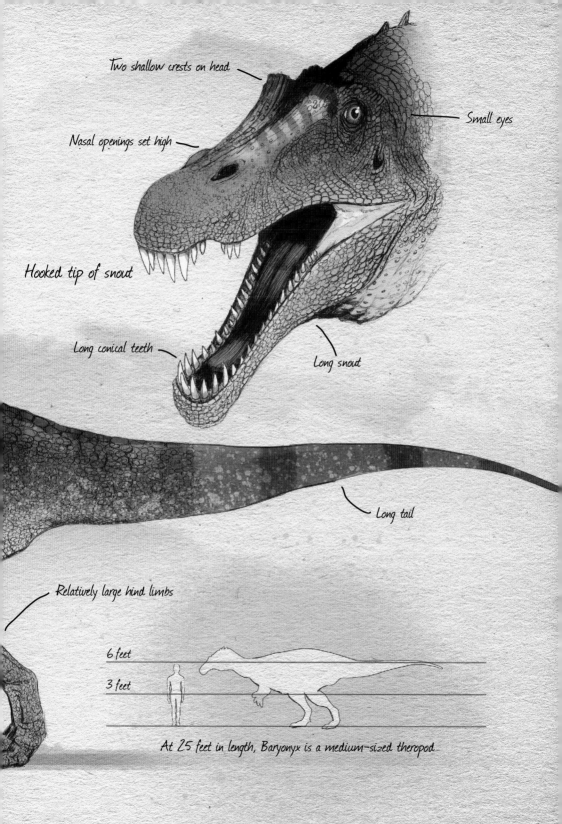

Two shallow crests on head

Small eyes

Nasal openings set high

Hooked tip of snout

Long conical teeth

Long snout

Long tail

Relatively large hind limbs

6 feet

3 feet

At 25 feet in length, Baryonyx is a medium-sized theropod.

Muscular arms with thick bones
used to secure prey

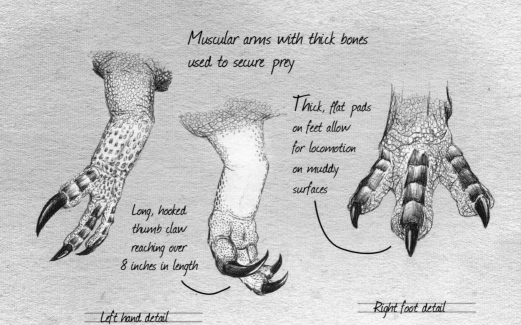

Thick, flat pads
on feet allow
for locomotion
on muddy
surfaces

Long, hooked
thumb claw
reaching over
8 inches in length

Left hand detail

Right foot detail

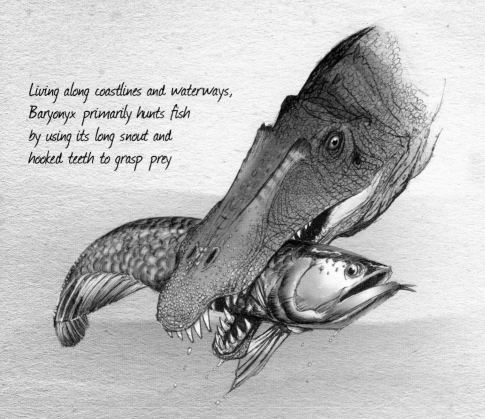

Living along coastlines and waterways,
Baryonyx primarily hunts fish
by using its long snout and
hooked teeth to grasp prey

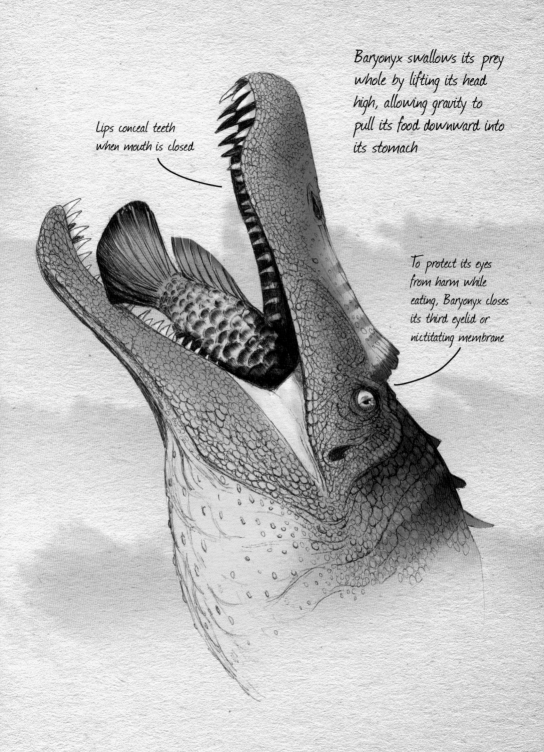

Lips conceal teeth
when mouth is closed

Baryonyx swallows its prey
whole by lifting its head
high, allowing gravity to
pull its food downward into
its stomach

To protect its eyes
from harm while
eating, Baryonyx closes
its third eyelid or
nictitating membrane

Beipiaosaurus inexpectus

Location Observed: Liaoning, China

Family: Therizinosauroidae

Length: 6 feet (2.2 meters)

Height: 3 feet (1 meter)

Weight: 90 lbs. (40 kg)

Temperament: Cautious, shy

Beipiaosaurus eats primarily grubs and small burrowing animals. It hunts using its claws to dig into decayed wood or soil and then plunging its hard beak into the hole to pull out its prey.

Hard tip used for digging

Long beak

Feathered crest on head

Small teeth

Curved jaw

Threat display

Pulls head up with mouth open

Spreads wings and claws outward to appear larger

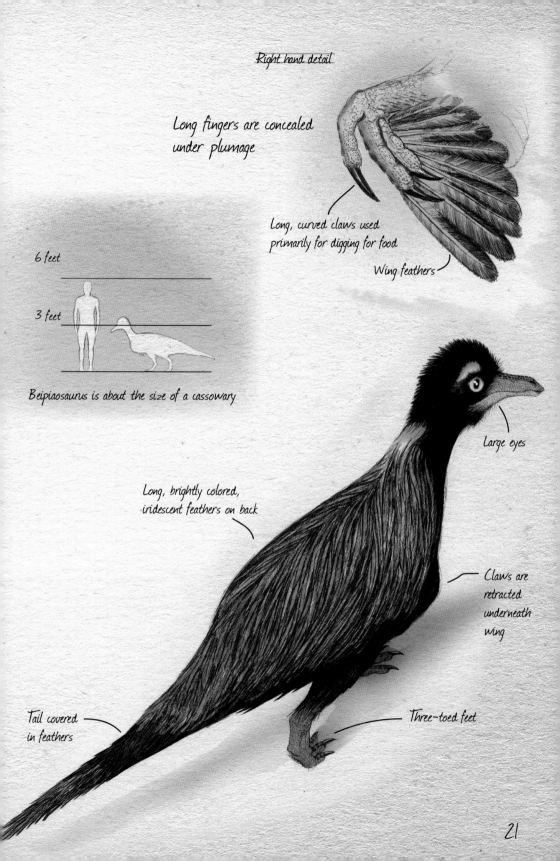

Right hand detail

Long fingers are concealed under plumage

Long, curved claws used primarily for digging for food

Wing feathers

6 feet

3 feet

Beipiaosaurus is about the size of a cassowary

Large eyes

Long, brightly colored, iridescent feathers on back

Claws are retracted underneath wing

Tail covered in feathers

Three-toed feet

Carcharodontosaurus saharicus

Location Observed: *Morocco, Africa*

Family: *Carcharodontosauridae*

Length: *40 feet (12 meters)*

Height: *13 feet (4 meters)*

Weight: *6 tons*

Temperament: *Extremely aggressive, solitary*

Small crest of dermal growth on head

Powerful arms and claws

Massive hind limbs

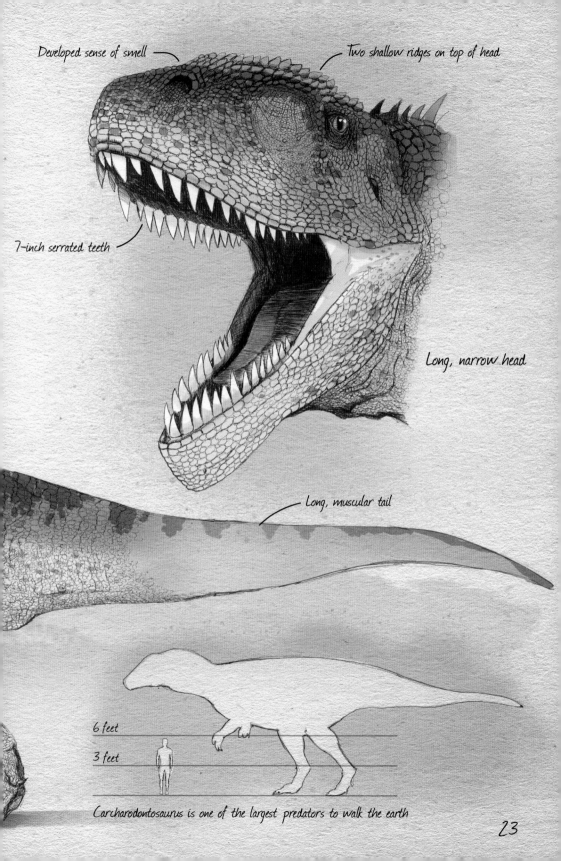

Developed sense of smell

Two shallow ridges on top of head

7-inch serrated teeth

Long, narrow head

Long, muscular tail

6 feet

3 feet

Carcharodontosaurus is one of the largest predators to walk the earth

Born covered in downy feathers for insulation

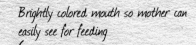
Brightly colored mouth so mother can easily see for feeding

Egg tooth used to break through egg shell

Carcharodontosaurus hatchling

Two weeks old

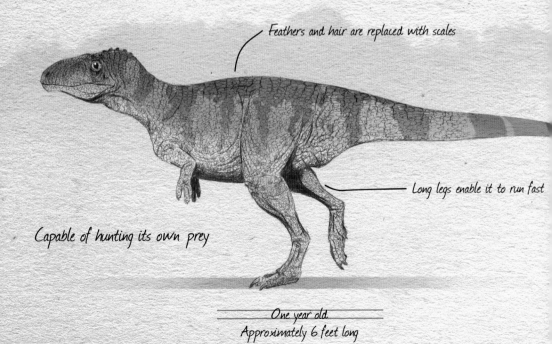

Feathers and hair are replaced with scales

Long legs enable it to run fast

Capable of hunting its own prey

One year old
Approximately 6 feet long

An adult is strong enough to
overpower prey twice its size
or take over another predator's kill

The apex predator of
its time, an adult
Carcharodontosaurus
has no rivals

Concavenator corcovatus

Location Observed: Cuenca, Spain

Family: Carcharodontosauridae

Length: 25 feet (7.5 meters)

Height: 9 feet (2.74 meters)

Weight: 1.2 tons

Temperament: Territorial, aggressive

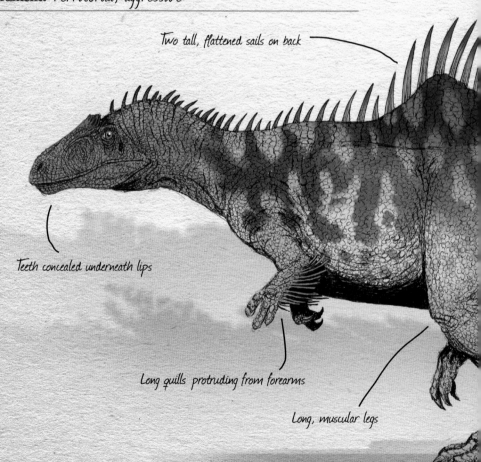

Two tall, flattened sails on back

Teeth concealed underneath lips

Long quills protruding from forearms

Long, muscular legs

Two crests over eyes

Low crest above nasal openings

Large, serrated teeth

Narrow jaw

Large jaw muscle

Long dermal spines along back

6 feet

3 feet

Hollow quills along forearms used as a mating display

Large razor-sharp claws for grasping prey

Using a burst of speed, Concavenator secures its prey with its arms and mouth

Pelecanimimus polyodon

28

When facing its prey,
Concavenator upresents
a narrow profile

29

Microraptor gui

Location Observed: Liaoning, China

Family: Dromaeosauridae

Length: 2.5 feet (.7 meter)

Height: 2.6 feet (.75 meter) wingspan

Weight: 1.3 lbs (.6 kg)

Temperament: Reclusive, cautious

Tail detail

Three claws on its hands

Large eyes to hunt at night
and in low-light conditions

Small teeth

Microraptor emits a high-pitched
squawk to warn others to stay
clear of its territory

Bright colors on tail ac
display to attract mate

3 feet

Microraptor is about the size of a hawk

Long forelimbs with
three-clawed hands

Primary flight feathers

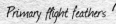

Microraptor glides for great distances,
allowing it to ambush prey without
giving away its position

Right forewing

Left hind wing

Microraptor's
primary
weapon is its
talons

Large sickle-like
claws on its feet

Wings on its legs

Long legs allow Microraptor to
spring into the air instantly to
avoid predators

Scipionyx samniticus

Location Observed: Central Italy

Family: Compsognathidae

Length: 5 feet (1.5 meters)

Height: 1.5 feet (.5 meters)

Weight: 6 lbs (2.6 Kg)

Temperament: Shy, elusive

Long snout

Long, slender body

Long neck

Three-fingered hands with sharp claws

Long legs designed to run fast

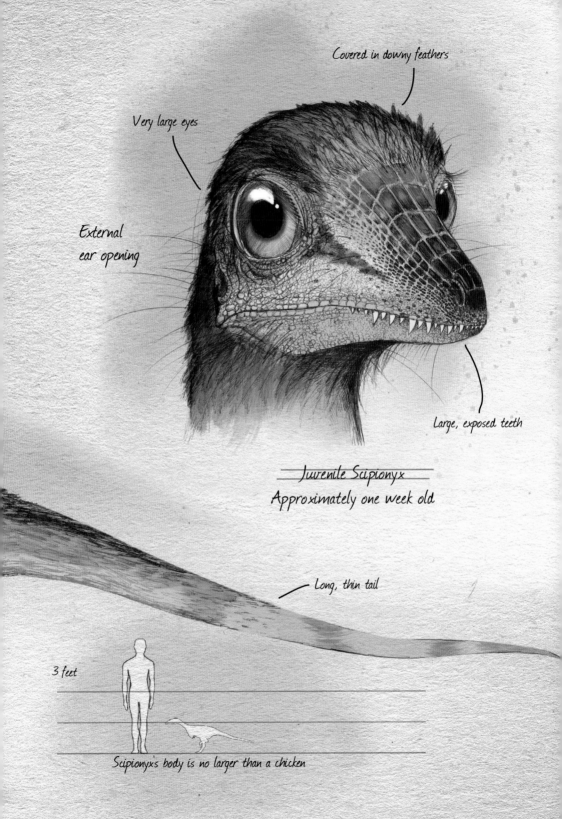

Covered in downy feathers

Very large eyes

External
ear opening

Large, exposed teeth

Juvenile Scipionyx
Approximately one week old

Long, thin tail

3 feet

Scipionyx's body is no larger than a chicken

Utahraptor ostrommaysorum

Location Observed: *Utah, United States*

Family: *Dromaeosauridae*

Length: *18 feet (5.5 meters)*

Height: *7 feet (2.1 meters)*

Weight: *600 lbs (272 Kg)*

Temperament: *Extremely aggressive*

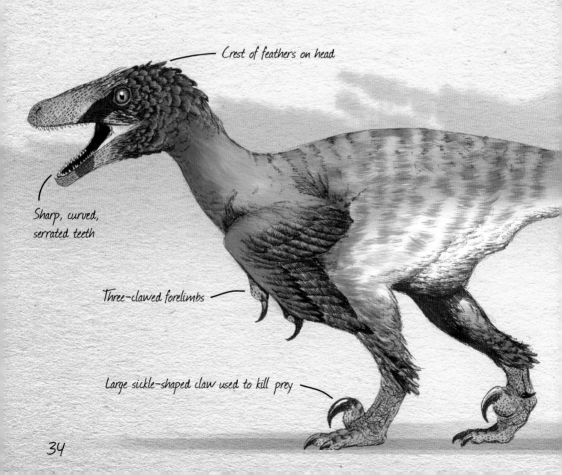

Crest of feathers on head

Sharp, curved, serrated teeth

Three-clawed forelimbs

Large sickle-shaped claw used to kill prey

Large, forward-facing eyes

Feathers cover entire body

Lips conceal teeth

Long, stiff tail

Feather display at end of tail

6 feet

3 feet

Utahraptor is the largest known raptor

Beneath the wing plumage
lies a deadly weapon

Three-clawed hands
designed for gripping and
holding prey

Utahraptor right wing detail

A Utahraptor pack
hunting an Iguanadon

Utahraptor hunts in packs

By isolating one animal from the herd, Utahraptor uses its speed and weapons to bring down prey much heavier than itself

Utahraptor's stiff tail acts as a counterbalance to shift its weight from one side to the other

Utahraptor's large killing claw is always kept in an upright position to prevent wear

Utahraptor left foot detail

Its short wings are used to keep its balance

Yutyrannus huali

Location Observed: Liaoning, China

Family: Tyrannosauroidea

Length: 30 feet (9 meters)

Height: 9.5 feet (3 meters)

Weight: 2.5 tons

Temperament: Aggressive, territorial, very social

Yutyrannus left foot

Feather-like fur covering its entire body, including the tail

Muscular arms with large claws for grabbing prey

Powerful legs

Yutyrannus left hand detail

Bony crest along the
top of its head

Two horns

Large, serrated teeth

Long, slender tail

6 feet

3 feet

Yutyrannus measures 30 feet from head to tail

39

The Pterosaurs

As you walk through the sand and approach a river basin, you feel a large shadow drape over you. You look up and see an enormous flying creature gliding toward the shore. It pulls its wings up and, with a powerful thrust, forces them downward as it climbs higher. It scans the surface of the water below and locks its eyes on something. Slowly pulling its wings in, it dives toward the water with incredible speed. Within inches of reaching the surface, it spreads its massive wings and slows down. It then breaks the calm water with its long head and pulls out a fish in a single sweeping motion. The hunt doesn't go unnoticed. Two more arrive just as large as the first. They create a commotion, squawking and flapping as they try to take the prey from its toothy beak. The aerial battle continues as they fly higher. Finally, one grasps the head of the fish, tearing it away. The hunter, left with half a fish, flies off leaving the other two to battle over the stolen half. You just witnessed the pterosaurs of the Early Cretaceous—some of the largest animals ever to take flight.

6 feet

3 feet

The pterosaur, meaning "winged lizard" in ancient Greek, is the earliest known vertebrate to evolve a means of self-powered flight. Although many people refer to them as dinosaurs, pterosaurs are in fact not dinosaurs, but belong to an order of animals informally classified as "flying reptiles." Very different than any flying animal living today, pterosaurs' wings consist of an elongated fourth finger with a fibrous membrane attaching the tip of the finger to the ankle of the hind leg. Their bodies are very small in comparison to their wings and head. All have air-filled, hollow bones with delicate skeletal structures. They are remarkably diverse in size; some have wingspans ranging from 10 inches, while others' reach over 30 feet—longer than a small aircraft.

Pterosaurs lived throughout most of the Mesozoic Era. The earliest species began to evolve in the Late Triassic period, with the latest going extinct at the end of the Cretaceous. The early pterosaurs had long tails and smaller heads and were smaller overall than later species. Pterosaurs' bodies were covered in a fine integument, or body covering, called "pycnofibres," which were similar to hair. Many, if not most, were piscatorial, meaning they hunted and fed on fish. Therefore some had developed long teeth designed to grasp and hold their prey. Others developed adaptations for feeding on small creatures along shorelines or hunting mid-air.

The Pterosaurs of the Early Cretaceous
By the Early Cretaceous period many species of pterosaurs had become significantly larger than their earlier ancestors. Their tails had reduced to a fraction of their original size, and their heads

had become massive. Many had heads the size of their necks and torsos combined. Large crests began to evolve. These were used as displays to attract mates or to show dominance over rivals. By this period, pterosaur species had spread around the world, from Africa to Europe to South America.

The two species outlined in this book are Anhanguera blittersdorffi and Tapejara imperator; both are from South America and fed on fish. One is an example of a toothed pterosaur, while the other is an example of a toothless pterosaur. The following pages examine the animals that ruled the skies of the Early Cretaceous.

Pterosaur wing

Membrane from elongated fourth finger forms wing

Modern bat wing

Membrane between fingers forms wing

Modern bird wing

Feathers extending from arm form wing

Anhanguera blittersdorffi

Location Observed: Brazil, South America

Family: Anhangueridae

Length: 15 feet (4.5 meters) wingspan

Height: 5 feet (1.5 meters) body length

Weight: 33 lbs (15 kg)

Temperament: Aggressive

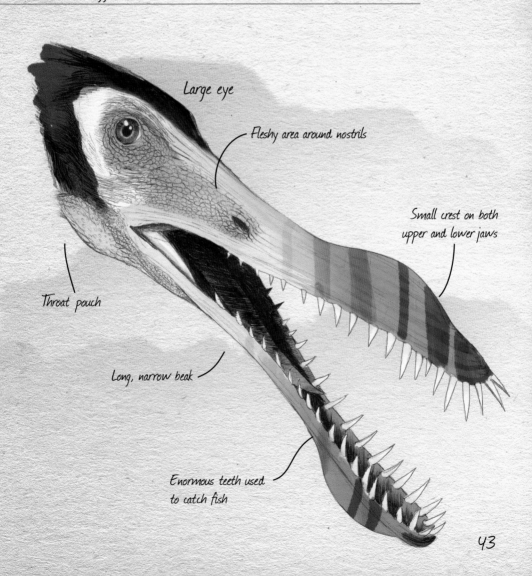

Large eye

Fleshy area around nostrils

Small crest on both upper and lower jaws

Throat pouch

Long, narrow beak

Enormous teeth used to catch fish

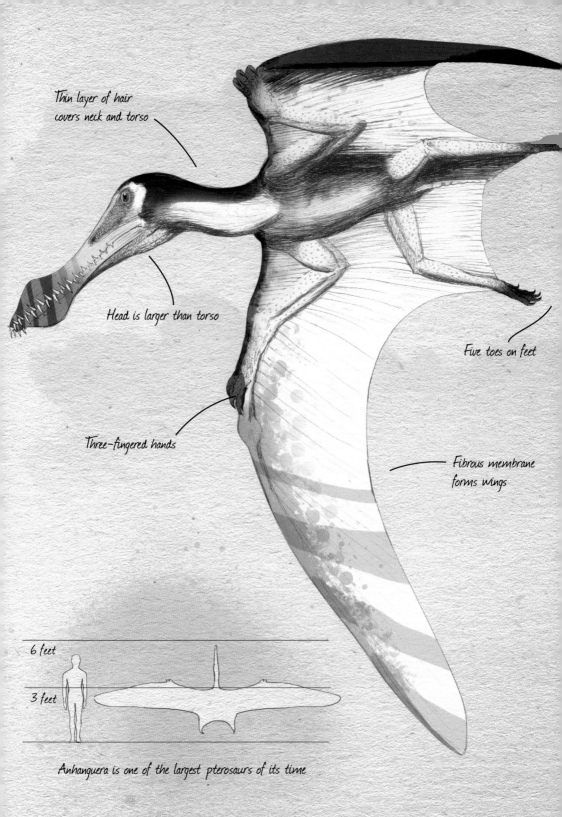

Thin layer of hair covers neck and torso

Head is larger than torso

Three-fingered hands

Five toes on feet

Fibrous membrane forms wings

6 feet

3 feet

Anhanguera is one of the largest pterosaurs of its time

44

Every meal was challenged. Anhanguera was also an paopportunist, taking prey from others in mid-flight.

Cladocyclus gardineri 3 feet (.9 meters)

Neoproscinetes penalvai 15 inches (.3 meters)

Tharrhias araripis 16 inches (.4 meters)

Tapejara imperator

Location Observed: *Brazil, South America*

Family: *Tapejaridae*

Length: *12 feet (3.6 meters) wingspan*

Height: *3 feet (.6 meters) crest height*

Weight: *26 lbs (12 kg)*

Temperament: *Social*

Male

Female

Fourth finger forms the wing

Right hand detail

Right foot detail

Large crest on head

Small crest on chin

Three-fingered hands

Four-toed feet

Tapejara's crest is about half the size of its body length

6 feet

3 feet

47

Pronunciation Key

Theropods (Theer-uh-pods)

Acrocanthosaurus atokensis (Ah-crow-can-tho-sore-uss, ah-toe-ken-sis)

Baryonyx walkeri (Barry-on-x, walk-kerry)

Beipiaosaurus inexpectus (Bay-pee-awo-sore-us, in-expec-tus)

Carcharodontosaurus saharicus (Kar-kar-odon-toe-sore-us, sa-harr-e-cuss)

Concavenator corcovatus (Con-ka-vee-nay-tor, cor-ko-vay-tus)

Microraptor gui (My-crow-rap-tor, gee)

Scipionyx samniticus (She-pee-on-x, sam-ni-ti-cuss)

Utahraptor ostrommaysorum (You-taw-rap-tor, ah-strom-ay-sore-um)

Yutyrannus huali (You-tee-ran-us, hual-ee)

Pterosaurs (Ter-uh-sore)

Anhanguera blittersdorffi (Ahn-han-gwera, blit-ters-dorf-eye)

Tapejara imperator (Tap-eh-jar-ah, em-par-ah-tor)

About the Authors

Juan Carlos Alonso

Juan Carlos Alonso (author and illustrator) is a Cuban American graphic designer, creative director, and illustrator. He has over 30 years experience in the graphic design/illustration field. In 1992 he founded Alonso & Company, a creative boutique specializing in branding, design, and advertising. His passion for nature has taken him around the world, from Australia to the Galapagos Islands, to study animals. Along with his work in the graphic arts, he is also an accomplished wildlife sculptor, focusing mostly on prehistoric animals.

Gregory S. Paul

Gregory S. Paul (co-author) is an American freelance researcher, author, and illustrator who works in paleontology. He is best known for his work and research on theropod dinosaurs and his detailed illustrations, both live and skeletal. Professionally investigating and restoring dinosaurs for three decades, Paul received an on-screen credit as a dinosaur specialist on *Jurassic Park* and Discovery Channel's *When Dinosaurs Roamed America* and *Dinosaur Planet*. He is the author and illustrator of *Predatory Dinosaurs of the World* (1988), *The Complete Illustrated Guide to Dinosaur Skeletons* (1996), *Dinosaurs of the Air* (2001), *The Princeton Field Guide To Dinosaurs* (2010), *Gregory S. Paul's Dinosaur Coffee Table Book* (2010), and editor of *The Scientific American Book of Dinosaurs* (2000). Paul has named over twelve prehistoric animal species and has had two dinosaur species named after him (*Cryptovolans pauli* and *Sellacoxa pauli*) based on his innovative theories.